Choice in Currency

A WAY TO STOP INFLATION

F. A. HAYEK

Nobel Laureate 1974

with Commentaries by
IVOR F. PEARCE • HAROLD B. ROSE
DOUGLAS JAY • SIR KEITH JOSEPH

Published by

THE INSTITUTE OF ECONOMIC AFFAIRS
1976

Republished in cooperation with
The Ludwig von Mises Institute
2009

Large Print Edition published 2013 by Skyler J. Collins.
Visit: www.skylerjcollins.com

First published by the Institute of Economic Affairs, London in 1976.

ISBN-13: 978-1494734930
ISBN-10: 1494734931

Contents

PREFACE .... *Arthur Seldon* 5

THE AUTHOR 8

I MONEY, KEYNES AND HISTORY 9
    Keynesian rehabilitation 10
    Personal confession 10

II THE MANUFACTURE OF UNEMPLOYMENT 11
    Unemployment via 'full employment policies' 12
    The lost generation 13
    The 1863 penny 13

III THE WEAKNESS OF POLITICAL CONTROL OF MONEY 14
    Group interests harmful 14
    Rebuilding the resistances to inflation 15
    Protecting money from politics 16
    A dangerous monopoly 16

IV CHOICE OF MONEY FOR PAYMENT IN CONTRACTS 17
    Government and legal tender 17
    Benefits of free currency system 19

V LONG-RUN MONETARY STABILITY 20
    'The universal prize' 20
    Free dealings in money better than monetary unions 21

A COMMENT ON KEYNES, BEVERIDGE AND KEYNESIAN ECONOMICS 23

COMMENTARIES:

    Professor Ivor Pearce...25
    Professor Harold Rose..26
    Rt. Hon. Douglas Jay..27
    Rt. Hon. Sir Keith Joseph...28

A NOTE ON GOVERNMENT MONOPOLY OF MONEY IN
   THEORY AND HISTORY ....*Sudha Shenoy*............30

    I. THEORY..30
    II. HISTORY...34

        France, 1789 34
        USA, before and after 1857...38
        Germany, 1920-23...39

AND A PORTENT...?
    Currency Option for Foreign Creditors....................................45

Preface

THE *Occasional Papers* are intended to make essays or addresses, of outstanding importance, accessible to a wider readership than that to which they were originally addressed. The 47 so far have included *Papers* by some of Britain's, and the world's, leading economists but also some important *Papers* by less well-known names.

No. 48 is an edited version of an address by Professor F. A. Hayek to a conference in Switzerland. In a sense it is a sequel to Occasional Paper 45, in which Professor Hayek argued that the cause of unemployment was not inadequate demand, arising from inadequate *total* income, but disproportions in relative wages required to equate the demand for labour and its supply *in each sector* of the economy. The error of supposing that full employment, high output and prosperity could be maintained by enlarging total money expenditure is described in this *Paper* as an age-old superstition to which Keynes and his followers have given the sanction of scientific authority.

In this *Paper* Professor Hayek considers the conditions under which it is possible for government to enlarge total expenditure by increasing the quantity of money. He argues that history indicates that, sooner or later, the control of the supply of money by government has ended in inflation. Hence the development of national and international monetary systems based on gold and other devices designed to remove from government the powers it invariably abused.

The opposite view, argued strongly in recent years in Britain, is that, if government was released from rigid mechanical rules in domestic or overseas monetary management, such as fixed exchange rates, it would be better able to act for the general good. This expectation, it is now evident, has not been realised because, although the rules were reasonably clear, government has found them politically tempting to break in practice. This is not a theoretical doubt whether government can improve on an automatic or semi-automatic monetary system, such as a gold or gold-exchange standard, in which the supply and value of money is beyond domestic political control. It is a practical judgement in political economy that a government subject to electoral pressures will not be able to observe the rules if to do so brings transitionary dislocation and unemployment.

Professor Hayek therefore argues that the time may have come to remove from government the power to require its citizens to use the money under its control. And in the last resort this would require that government be deprived of the power to define legal tender. The requirement is not to deprive government of the power to issue money but to deny it the exclusive right to do so and to force the citizenry to use it at the price it specifies. It is thus the government monopoly of money that is objectionable, and history is full of examples of governments that have attempted to enforce their power by extreme measures, including the ultimate sanction of death.

The solution is therefore to allow people to use the money they find most convenient, whether the money issued by their own government or by other governments. Professor Hayek argues that this system would be more desirable and practicable than a utopian European Monetary Unit.

This proposal, Professor Hayek recognises, may seem far-fetched after centuries in which it has been considered that one of the proper, or essential, functions of government is to provide a currency on which the citizens could depend as a reliable unit of account and means of exchange, a function which has included the concept of legal tender. Professor Hayek denies that legal tender is an essential part of the monetary function of government. He argues that people should be free to refuse money they distrust in favour of money in which they have confidence. It is this new power of the people to refuse the national money that would induce national governments to ensure that their money was stable in value. Hence Professor Hayek argues the case for a new kind of international money.

In this *Occasional Paper* Professor Hayek has provided stimulating analysis of a contemporary problem and emerged with a radical solution. He considers ways in which the system might work in practice, and replies to objections to it. He discusses the effects it will have on banking systems, and in so doing he provides a commentary on the current debate on money and inflation and on the desired national and international institutions. Here it will come as no surprise to learn that he believes an international monetary authority is hardly to be trusted more than a national authority: he would confine government to 'a framework of legal roles in which the people could develop the monetary institutions that best suit them'.

To indicate the possibly varying views on the importance and the practicality of Professor Hayek's proposals we invited comments from two economists and two senior politicians who have held high government office. The economists are Professor Ivor Pearce and Professor Harold Rose. Both politicians, Mr Douglas Jay and Sir Keith Joseph, are Fellows of All Souls College, Oxford, and are especially interested in economic affairs.

To illustrate the argument Miss Sudha Shenoy has assembled extracts from economic and historical writings on the failure of governments in France and Germany to confine the use of money to legal tender despite severe penalties and on the fall in the value of paper legal tender as its supply was increased during periods of inflation, and on the exclusion by the US Government of currencies other than the dollar.

November 1975   ARTHUR SELDON

The Author

FRIEDRICH AUGUST HAYEK, Dr Jur, Dr Sc Pol (Vienna), DSc (Econ.) (London), Visiting Professor at the University of Salzburg, Austria, 1970-74. Educated at the University of Vienna, Director of the Austrian Institute for Economic Research, 1927-31, and Lecturer in Economics at the University of Vienna, 1929-31. 1931-50 Tooke Professor of Economic Science and Statistics, University of London. 1950-62 Professor of Social and Moral Science, University of Chicago. Professor of Economics, University of Freiburg i.Brg., West Germany, 1962-68. He was awarded the Alfred Nobel Memorial Prize in Economic Sciences in 1974.

Professor Hayek's most important publications include *Monetary Theory and the Trade Cycle* (1933), *The Pure Theory of Capital* (1941), *The Road to Serfdom* (1944), *Individualism and Economic Order* (1948), *The Counter-Revolution of Science.* (1952), and *The Constitution of Liberty* (1960). His latest works are collections of his writings under the titles *Studies in Philosophy, Politics and Economics* (1967) and *Law, Legislation and Liberty* (Vol. I, 1973). He has also edited several books and has published articles in the *Economic Journal, Economica* and other journals. The IEA has published his *The Confusion of Language in Political Thought* (Occasional Paper *20,* 1968), his Wincott Memorial Lecture, *Economic Freedom and Representative Government* (Occasional Paper 39, 1973), a collection of his writings with a new essay (assembled by Sudha Shenoy), *A Tiger by the Tail* (Hobart Paperback 4, 1972), an essay in *Verdict on Rent Control* (IEA Readings NO.7, 1972), and *Full Employment at Any Price?* (Occasional Paper 45, 1975).

Choice in Currency: A Way to Stop Inflation[1]

F.A.HAYEK

I.
MONEY, KEYNES AND HISTORY[2]

THE CHIEF ROOT of our present monetary troubles is, of course, the sanction of scientific authority which Lord Keynes and his disciples have given to the age-old superstition that by increasing the aggregate of money expenditure we can lastingly ensure prosperity and full employment. It is a superstition against which economists before Keynes had struggled with some success for at least two centuries.[3] It had governed most of earlier history. This history, indeed, has been largely a history of inflation; significantly, it was only during the rise of the prosperous modern industrial systems and during the rule of the gold standard, that over a period of about two hundred years (in Britain from about 1714 to 1914, and in the United States from about 1749 to 1939) prices were at the end about where they had been at the beginning. During this unique period of monetary stability the gold standard had imposed upon monetary authorities a discipline which prevented them from abusing their powers, as they have done

---

[1] Based on an Address entitled 'International Money' delivered to the Geneva Gold and Monetary Conference on 25 September, 1975, at Lausanne, Switzerland.

[2] [The main section and sub-headings have been inserted to help readers, especially non-economists unfamiliar with Professor Hayek's writings, to follow the argument; they were not part of the original lecture.-ED.]

[3] [This observation is amplified by Professor Hayek in a note, 'A Comment on Keynes, Beveridge and Keynesian Economics', page 23.-ED.]

at nearly all other times. Experience in other parts of the world does not seem to have been very different: I have been told that a Chinese law attempted to prohibit paper money for all times (of course, ineffectively), long before the Europeans ever invented it!

Keynesian rehabilitation

It was John Maynard Keynes, a man of great intellect but limited knowledge of economic theory, who ultimately succeeded in rehabilitating a view long the preserve of cranks with whom he openly sympathised. He had attempted by a succession of new theories to justify the same, superficially persuasive, intuitive belief that had been held by many practical men before, but that will not withstand rigorous analysis of the price mechanism: just as there cannot be a uniform price for all kinds of labour, an equality of demand and supply for labour in general cannot be secured by managing *aggregate* demand. The volume of employment depends on the correspondence of demand and supply *in each sector* of the economy, and therefore on the wage structure and the distribution of demand between the sectors. The consequence is that over a longer period the Keynesian remedy does not cure unemployment but makes it worse.

The claim of an eminent public figure and brilliant polemicist to provide a cheap and easy means of permanently preventing serious unemployment conquered public opinion and, after his death, professional opinion too. Sir John Hicks has even proposed that we call the third quarter of this century, 1950 to 1975, the age of Keynes, as the second quarter was the age of Hitler.[1] I do not feel that the harm Keynes did is really so much as to justify *that* description. But it is true that, so long as his prescriptions seemed to work, they operated as an orthodoxy which it appeared useless to oppose.

Personal confession

I have often blamed myself for having given up the struggle after I had spent much time and energy criticising the first version of Keynes's theoretical framework. Only after the second part of my critique had appeared did he tell me he had

---

[1] John Hicks, *The Crisis in Keynesian Economics*, Oxford University Press, 1974, p.1.

changed his mind and no longer believed what he had said in the *Treatise on Money* of 1930 (somewhat unjustly towards himself, as it seems to me, since I still believe that volume II of the *Treatise* contains some of the best work he ever did). At any rate, I felt it then to be useless to return to the charge, because he seemed so likely to change his views again. When it proved that this new version - the *General Theory* of 1936 - conquered most of the professional opinion, and when in the end even some of the colleagues I most respected supported the wholly Keynesian Bretton Woods agreement, I largely withdrew from the debate, since to proclaim my dissent from the near-unanimous views of the orthodox phalanx would merely have deprived me of a hearing on other matters about which I was more concerned at the time. (I believe, however, that, so far as some of the best British economists were concerned, their support of Bretton Woods was determined more by a misguided patriotism - the hope that it would benefit Britain in her post-war difficulties - than by a belief that it would provide a satisfactory international monetary order.)

II

THE MANUFACTURE OF UNEMPLOYMENT

I WROTE 36 years ago on the crucial point of difference:

> 'It may perhaps be pointed out that it has, of course, never been denied that employment can be rapidly increased, and a position of "full employment" achieved in the shortest possible time, by means of monetary expansion - least of all by those economists whose outlook has been influenced by the experience of a major inflation. All that has been contended is that the kind of full employment which can be created in this way is inherently unstable, and that to create employment by these means is to perpetuate fluctuations. There may be desperate situations in which it may indeed be necessary to increase employment at all costs, even if it be only for a short period - perhaps the situation in which Dr Brüning found himself in Germany in 1932 was such a situation in which desperate means would have been justified. But the economist should not conceal the fact that to

aim at the maximum of employment which can be achieved in the short run by means of monetary policy is essentially the policy of the desperado who has nothing to lose and everything to gain from a short breathing space.'[1]

To this I would now like to add, in reply to the constant deliberate misrepresentation of my views by politicians, who like to picture me as a sort of bogey whose influence makes conservative parties dangerous, what I regularly emphasize and stated nine months ago in my Nobel Memorial Prize Lecture at Stockholm in the following words:

> 'The truth is that by a mistaken theoretical view we have been led into a precarious position in which we cannot prevent substantial unemployment from re-appearing: not because, as my view is sometimes misrepresented, this unemployment is deliberately brought about as a means to combat inflation, but because it is now bound to appear as a deeply regrettable but *inescapable* consequence of the mistaken policies of the past as soon as inflation ceases to accelerate.'[2]

Unemployment via 'full employment policies'
This manufacture of unemployment by what are called 'full employment policies' is a complex process. In essence it operates by temporary changes in the distribution of demand, drawing both unemployed and already employed workers into jobs which will disappear with the end of inflation. In the periodically recurrent crises of the pre-1914 years the expansion of credit during the preceding boom served largely to finance industrial investment, and the over-development and subsequent unemployment occurred mainly in the industries producing capital equipment. In the engineered inflation of the last decades things were more complex.

What will happen during a major inflation is illustrated by

---

[1] F.A. Hayek, *Profits, Interest and Investment*, Routledge & Kegan Paul, London, 1939, p. 63n.

[2] F.A. Hayek, 'The Pretence of Knowledge', Nobel Memorial Prize Lecture 1974, reprinted in *Full Employment at Any Price?*, Occasional Paper 45, IEA, 1975, p. 37.

an observation from the early 1920s which many of my Viennese contemporaries will confirm: in the city many of the famous coffee houses were driven from the best corner sites by new bank offices and returned after the 'stabilization crisis', when the banks had contracted or collapsed and thousands of bank clerks swelled the ranks of the unemployed.

The lost generation
The whole theory underlying the full employment policies has by now of course been thoroughly discredited by the experience of the last few years. In consequence the economists are also beginning to discover its fatal intellectual defects which they ought to have seen all along. Yet I fear the theory will still give us a lot of trouble: it has left us with a lost generation of economists who have learnt nothing else. One of our chief problems will be to protect our money against those economists who will continue to offer their quack remedies, the short-term effectiveness of which will continue to ensure them popularity. It will survive among blind doctrinaires who have always been convinced that they have the key to salvation.

The 1863 penny
In consequence, though the rapid descent of Keynesian doctrine from intellectual respectability can be denied no longer, it still gravely threatens the chances of a sensible monetary policy. Nor have people yet fully realised how much irreparable damage it has already done, particularly in Britain, the country of its origin. The sense of financial respectability which once guided British monetary policy has rapidly disappeared. From a model to be imitated Britain has in a few years descended to be a warning example for the rest of the world. This decay was recently brought home to me by a curious incident: I found in a drawer of my desk a British penny dated 1863 which a short 12 years ago, that is, when it was exactly a hundred years old, I had received as change from a London bus conductor and had taken back to Germany to show to my students what long-run monetary stability meant. I believe they were duly impressed. But they would laugh in my face if I now mentioned Britain as an instance of monetary stability.

III
THE WEAKNESS OF POLITICAL CONTROL OF MONEY

A WISE MAN should perhaps have foreseen that less than 30 years after the nationalisation of the Bank of England the purchasing power of the pound sterling would have been reduced to less than one-quarter of what it had been at that date. As has sooner or later happened everywhere, government control of the quantity of money has once again proved fatal. I do not want to question that a very intelligent and wholly independent national or international monetary authority *might* do better than an international gold standard, or any other sort of automatic system. But I see not the slightest hope that any government, or any institution subject to political pressure, will ever be able to act in such a manner.

Group interests harmful
I never had much illusion in this respect, but I must confess that in the course of a long life my opinion of governments has steadily worsened: the more intelligently they try to act (as distinguished from simply following an established rule), the more harm they seem to do - because once they are known to aim at particular goals (rather than merely maintaining a self-correcting spontaneous order) the less they can avoid serving sectional interests. And the demands of all organised group interests are almost invariably harmful - except only when they protest against restrictions imposed upon them for the benefit of other group interests. I am by no means re-assured by the fact that, at least in some countries, the civil servants who run affairs are mostly intelligent, well-meaning, and honest men. The point is that, if governments are to remain in office in the prevailing political order, they have no choice but to use their powers for the benefit of particular groups - and one strong interest is always to get additional money for extra expenditure. However harmful inflation is in general seen to be, there are always substantial groups of people, including some for whose support collectivist-inclined governments primarily look, which in the short run greatly gain by it - even if only by staving off for some time the loss of an income which it is human nature to believe

will be only temporary if they can tide over the emergency.

Rebuilding the resistances to inflation
The pressure for more and cheaper money is an ever-present political force which monetary authorities have never been able to resist, unless they were in a position credibly to point to an absolute obstacle which made it impossible for them to meet such demands. And it will become even more irresistible when these interests can appeal to an increasingly unrecognisable image of St Maynard. There will be no more urgent need than to erect new defenses against the onslaughts of popular forms of Keynesianism, that is, to replace or restore those restraints which, under the influence of his theory, have been systematically dismantled. It was the main function of the gold standard, of balanced budgets, of the necessity for deficit countries to contract their circulation, and of the limitation of the supply of 'international liquidity', to make it impossible for the monetary authorities to capitulate to the pressure for more money. And it was exactly for that reason that all these safeguards against inflation, which had made it possible for representative governments to resist the demands of powerful pressure groups for more money, have been removed at the instigation of economists who imagined that, if governments were released from the shackles of mechanical rules, they would be able to act wisely for the general benefit.

I do not believe we can now remedy this position by *constructing* some new international monetary order, whether a new international monetary authority or institution, or even an international agreement to adopt a particular mechanism or system of policy, such as the classical gold standard. I am fairly convinced that any attempt now to re-instate the gold standard by international agreement would break down within a short time and merely discredit the ideal of an international gold standard for even longer. Without the conviction of the public at large that certain immediately painful measures are occasionally necessary to preserve reasonable stability, we cannot hope that any authority which has power to determine the quantity of money will long resist the pressure for, or the seduction of, cheap money.

Protecting money from politics

The politician, acting on a modified Keynesian maxim that in the long run we are all out of office, does not care if his successful cure of unemployment is bound to produce more unemployment in the future. The politicians who will be blamed for it will not be those who created the inflation but those who stopped it. No worse trap could have been set for a democratic system in which the government is forced to act on the beliefs that the people think to be true. Our only hope for a stable money is indeed now to find a way to protect money from politics.

With the exception only of the 2oo-year period of the gold standard, practically all governments of history have used their exclusive power to issue money in order to defraud and plunder the people. There is less ground than ever for hoping that, so long as the people have no choice but to use the money their government provides, governments will become more trustworthy. Under the prevailing systems of government, which are supposed to be guided by the opinion of the majority but under which in practice any sizeable group may create a 'political necessity' for the government by threatening to withhold the votes it needs to claim majority support, we cannot entrust dangerous instruments to it. Fortunately we need not yet fear, I hope, that governments will start a war to please some indispensable group of supporters, but money is certainly too dangerous an instrument to leave to the fortuitous expediency of politicians - or, it seems. economists.

A dangerous monopoly

What is so dangerous and ought to be done away with is not governments' right to issue money but the *exclusive* right to do so and their power to force people to use it and to accept it at a particular price. This monopoly of government, like the postal monopoly, has its origin not in any benefit it secures for the people but solely in the desire to enhance the coercive powers of government. I doubt whether it has ever done any good except to the rulers and their favorites. All history contradicts the belief that governments have given us a safer money than we would have had without their claiming an exclusive right to issue it.

IV

CHOICE OF MONEY FOR PAYMENT IN CONTRACTS

BUT WHY should we not let people choose freely what money they want to use? By 'people' I mean the individuals who ought to have the right to decide whether they want to buy or sell for francs, pounds, dollars, D-marks, or ounces of gold. I have no objection to governments issuing money, but I believe their claim to a *monopoly,* or their power to *limit* the kinds of money in which contracts may be concluded within their territory, or to determine the *rates* at which monies can be exchanged, to be wholly harmful.

At this moment it seems that the best thing we could wish governments to do is for, say, all the members of the European Economic Community, or, better still, all the governments of the Atlantic Community, to bind themselves mutually not to place any restrictions on the free use within their territories of one another's - or any other - currencies, including their purchase and sale at any price the parties decide upon, or on their use as accounting units in which to keep books. This, and not a utopian European Monetary Unit, seems to me now both the practicable and the desirable arrangement to aim at. To make the scheme effective it would be important, for reasons I state later, also to provide that banks in one country be free to establish branches in any of the others.

Government and legal tender

This suggestion may at first seem absurd to all brought up on the concept of 'legal tender'. Is it not essential that the law designate one kind of money as the legal money? This is, however, true only to the extent that, *if* the government does issue money, it must also say what must be accepted in discharge of debts incurred in that money. And it must also determine in what manner certain non-contractual legal obligations, such as taxes or liabilities for damage or torts, are to be discharged. But there is no reason whatever why people should not be free to make contracts, including ordinary purchases and sales, in any kind of money they choose, or why they should be obliged to sell against any particular kind of money.

There could be no more effective check against the abuse of money by the government than if people were free to refuse any money they distrusted and to prefer money in which they had confidence. Nor could there be a stronger inducement to governments to ensure the stability of their money than the knowledge that, so long as they kept the supply below the demand for it, that demand would tend to grow. Therefore, let us deprive governments (or their monetary authorities) of all power to protect their money against competition: if they can no longer conceal that their money is becoming bad, they will have to restrict the issue.

The first reaction of many readers may be to ask whether the effect of such a system would not according to an old rule be that the bad money would drive out the good. But this would be a misunderstanding of what is called Gresham's Law. This indeed is one of the oldest insights into the mechanism of money, so old that 2,400 years ago Aristophanes, in one of his comedies, could say that it was with politicians as it is with coins, because the bad ones drive out the good.[1] But the truth which apparently even today is not generally understood is that Gresham's Law operates *only* if the two kinds of money have to be accepted at a prescribed rate of exchange. Exactly the opposite will happen when people are free to exchange the different kinds of money at whatever rate they can agree upon. This was observed many times during the great inflations when even the most severe penalties threatened by governments could not prevent people from using other kinds of money - even commodities like cigarettes and bottles of brandy

---

[1] Aristophanes, *Frogs,* 891-898, in Frere's translation:
Oftentimes we have reflected on a similar abuse
In the choice of men for office, and of coins for common use,
For our old and standard pieces, valued and approved and tried,
Here among the Grecian nations, and in all the world besides,
Recognised in every realm for trusty stamp and pure assay,
Are rejected and abandoned for the trash of yesterday,
For a vile adulterated issue, drossy, counterfeit and base,
Which the traffic of the city passes current in their place.
About the same time, the philosopher Diogenes called money 'the legislators' game of dice'!

rather than the government money - which clearly meant that the good money was driving out the bad.[1]

Benefits of free currency system

Make it merely legal and people will be very quick indeed to refuse to use the national currency once it depreciates noticeably, and they will make their dealings in a currency they trust. Employers, in particular, would find it in their interest to offer, in collective agreements, not wages anticipating a foreseen rise of prices but wages in a currency they trusted and could make the basis of rational calculation. This would deprive government of the power to counteract excessive wage increases, and the unemployment they would cause, by depreciating their currency. It would also prevent employers from conceding such wages in the expectation that the national monetary authority would bail them out if they promised more than they could pay.

There is no reason to be concerned about the effects of such an arrangement on ordinary men who know neither how to handle nor how to obtain strange kinds of money. So long as the shopkeepers knew that they could turn it instantly at the current rate of exchange into whatever money they preferred, they would be *only* too ready to sell their wares at an appropriate price for any currency. But the malpractices of government would show themselves much more rapidly if prices rose *only* in terms of the money issued by it, and people would soon learn to hold the government responsible for the value of the money in which they were paid. Electronic calculators, which in seconds would give the equivalent of any price in any currency at the current rate, would soon be used everywhere. But, unless the national government all too badly mismanaged the currency it issued, it would probably be continued to be used in everyday retail transactions. What would be affected mostly would be not so much the use of money in daily payments as the willingness to *hold* different kinds of money. It would mainly be the tendency of all business and capital transactions rapidly to switch to a

---

[1] During the German inflation after the First World War, when people began to use dollars and other solid currencies in the place of marks, a Dutch financier (if I rightly remember, Mr Vissering) asserted that Gresham's Law was false and the opposite is true.

more reliable standard (and to base calculations and accounting on it) which would keep national monetary policy on the right path.

V
LONG-RUN MONETARY STABILITY

THE UPSHOT would probably be that the currencies of those countries trusted to pursue a responsible monetary policy would tend to displace gradually those of a less reliable character. The reputation of financial righteousness would become a jealously guarded asset of all issuers of money, since they would know that even the slightest deviation from the path of honesty would reduce the demand for their product.

I do not believe there is any reason to fear that in such a competition for the most general acceptance of a currency there would arise a tendency to deflation or an increasing value of money. People will be quite as reluctant to borrow or incur debts in a currency expected to appreciate as they will hesitate to lend in a currency expected to depreciate. The convenience of use is decidedly in favour of a currency which can be expected to retain an approximately stable value. If governments and other issuers of money have to compete in inducing people to *hold* their money, and make long-term contracts in it, they will have to create confidence in its long-run stability.

'The universal prize'

Where I am not sure is whether in such a competition for reliability any government-issued currency would prevail, or whether the predominant preference would not be in favour of some such units as ounces of gold. It seems not unlikely that gold would ultimately re-assert its place as 'the universal prize in all countries, in all cultures, in all ages', as Jacob Bronowski has recently called it in his brilliant book on *The Ascent of Man*,[1] if people were given complete freedom to decide what to use as their standard and general medium of exchange - more likely, at any rate, than as the result of any organized attempt to restore the gold standard.

The reason why, in order to be fully effective, the free

---

[1] Jacob Bronowski, *The Ascent of Man*, BBC Publications, London 1973.

international market in currencies should extend also to the services of banks is, of course, that bank deposits subject to cheque represent today much the largest part of the liquid assets of most people. Even during the last hundred years or so of the gold standard this circumstance increasingly prevented it from operating as a fully international currency, because any inflow or outflow in or out of a country required a proportionate expansion or contraction of the much larger super-structure of the national credit money, the effect of which falls indiscriminately on the whole economy instead of merely increasing or decreasing the demand for the particular goods which was required to bring about a new balance between imports and exports. With a truly international banking system money could be transferred directly without producing the harmful process of secondary contractions or expansions of the credit structure.

It would probably also impose the most effective discipline on governments if they felt immediately the effects of their policies on the attractiveness of investment in their country. I have *just* read in an English Whig tract more than 250 years old: 'Who would establish a Bank in an arbitrary country, or trust his money constantly there?'[1] The tract, incidentally, tells us that yet another 50 years earlier a great French banker, Jean Baptist Tavernier, invested all the riches he had amassed in his long rambles over the world in what the authors described as 'the barren rocks of Switzerland'; when asked why by Louis XIV, he had the courage to tell him that 'he was willing to have something which he could call his own!' Switzerland, apparently, laid the foundations of her prosperity earlier than most people realise.

Free dealings in money better than monetary unions
I prefer the freeing of all dealings in money to any sort of monetary union also because the latter would demand an international monetary authority which I believe is neither practicable nor even desirable - and hardly to be more trusted than a national authority. It seems to me that there is a very sound element in the widespread disinclination to confer sovereign powers, or at least powers to command, on any

---

[1] Thomas Gordon and John Trenchard, *The Cato Letters*, letters dated 12 May, 1722, and 3 February, 1721 respectively, published in collected editions, London, 1724, and later.

international authority. What we need are not international authorities possessing powers of direction, but merely international bodies (or, rather, international treaties which are effectively enforced) which can prohibit certain actions of governments that will harm other people. Effectively to prohibit all restrictions on dealings in (and the possession of) different kinds of money (or claims for money) would at last make it possible that the absence of tariffs, or other obstacles to the movement of goods and men, will secure a genuine free trade area or common market - and do more than anything else to create confidence in the countries committing themselves to it. It is now urgently needed to counter that monetary nationalism that I first criticized almost 40 years ago[1] and which is becoming even more dangerous when, as a consequence of the close kinship between the two views, it is turning into monetary socialism. I hope it will not be too long before complete freedom to deal in any money one likes will be regarded as the essential mark of a free country.[2]

You may feel that my proposal amounts to no less than the abolition of monetary policy; and you would not be quite wrong. As in other connections, I have come to the conclusion that the best the state can do with respect to money is to provide a framework of legal rules within which the people can develop the monetary institutions that best suit them. It seems to me that if we could prevent governments from meddling with money, we would do more good than any government has ever done in this regard. And private enterprise would probably have done better than the best they have ever done.

---

[1] *Monetary Nationalism and International Stability*, Longmans, London, 1937.

[2] It may at first seem as if this suggestion were in conflict with my general support of fixed exchange rates under the present system. But this is not so. Fixed exchange rates seem to me to be necessary so long as national governments have a monopoly of issuing money in their territory in order to place them under a very necessary discipline. But this is of course no longer necessary when they have to submit to the discipline of competition with other issuers of money equally current within their territory.

A Comment on Keynes, Beveridge, and Keynesian Economics

LORD KEYNES has always appeared to me a kind of new John Law. Like Law, Keynes was a financial genius who made some real contributions to the theory of money. (Apart from an interesting and original discussion of the factors determining the value of money, Law gave the first satisfactory account of the cumulative growth of acceptability once a commodity was widely used as a medium of exchange.) But Keynes could never free himself from the popular false belief that, as Law expressed it, 'as the additional money will give work to people who were idle and enabled those already working to earn more, the output will increase and industry will prosper'.[1]

It was against this sort of view that Richard Cantillon and David Hume began the development of modern monetary theory. Hume in particular put the central point at issue by saying that, in the process of inflation, 'it is only in this interval or intermediate situation between the acquisition of money and the rise of prices, that the increasing quantity of gold and silver is favourable to industry'.[2] It is this work we shall have to do again after the Keynesian flood.

In one sense, however, it would be somewhat unfair to blame Lord Keynes too much for the developments after his death. I am certain he would have been - whatever he had said earlier - a leader in the fight against the present inflation. But

---

[1] John Law, *Money and Trade Considered with a Proposal for Supplying the Nations with Money*, W. Lewis, London, 1705. [*A Collection of Scarce and Valuable Tracts* (the Somers Collection of Tracts, Vol. XIII), John Murray, London, 1815, includes John Law's tract (1720 edition) at pp. 775-817; an extract from p. 812 reads: 'But as this addtion to the money will employ the people that are now idle, and those now employed to more advantage, so the product will be increased, and manufacture advanced.'- ED.]

[2] David Hume, *On Money* (Essay III).

developments, at least in Britain, were also mainly determined by the version of Keynesianism published under the name of Lord Beveridge for which (since he himself understood no economics whatever) his scientific advisers must bear the responsibility.

I have been blamed for charging Lord Keynes with a somewhat limited knowledge of economic theory, but the defectiveness of his views on the theory of international trade, for example, have often been pointed out. And the clearest proof seems to me to be the caricature of other theories which he presented, presumably in good faith, in order to refute them.

F.A.H.

Commentaries

IVOR PEARCE
Professor of Economics and Head of Department, University of Southampton, 1962-72
Director of Research, Econometric Model Building Unit, University of Southampton, 1973-75
Author of *A Model of Output, Employment, Wages and Prices in the UK (1976)*

IF I HAD the temerity, which I do not, to claim the existence of a fault in Professor Hayek's superb *Choice in Currency,* it would be a fault of omission rather than commission. Professor Hayek correctly identifies the secret of Keynes's success with a pseudo-exact 'sanction of scientific authority', but he does not explain in the same pseudo-exact terms the precise point of the neo-Keynesian error. Until this is done the 'lost generation' who were taught nothing but Keynes may very well remain unconvinced. Being myself one of the lost generation, now enlightened, I offer the following argument.

Neo-Keynesians hold that the act of saving takes money out of the circulation flow - income to purchases to income - whilst the act of investment adds money to that flow. To maintain a constant rate of flow, that is, a steady demand for goods, it is necessary that desired saving should equal desired investment. According to the Keynesian argument saving will vary with the level of employment, so that changes in the level of employment serve as a mechanism equating saving and investment. But, if this *is* the mechanism, the desire to save may be matched with the desire to invest at a level of employment less than full. The apparent remedy is to print and give away money to spend or to invest, that is, to stimulate artificially the desire to spend or to invest.

But the truth is that the act of saving does not ordinarily hold up the circular flow of money at all. If I choose to save more, I buy a bond with my new savings, an act which is possible only if someone sells a bond. The money I have saved is immediately available to the seller of the bond to buy goods. There is no failure of demand. A failure of demand occurs only if someone chooses *not* to pass the money on but to hold a larger stock of money than usual.

This will cause unemployment. But such unemployment must be transient. No part of the stock of money is destroyed. Failing some fundamental change in institutional conventions the very sum hoarded will eventually be released and demand restored. If, at the moment of each transient failure of demand, governments rush to create and put into circulation new money in accordance with the Keynesian prescription, inflation will occur as soon as the temporary hold-up in the flow of the old money ceases.

Nor is this the worst of it. Keynesian theory affords a cloak of respectability to acts of currency debasement formerly universally recognised as evil. The very institution - the British Parliament - originally founded to control the monetary excesses of the Sovereign, itself now engages in acts of currency debasement far beyond any thing that Henry VIII could have imagined, much less planned and executed. The watchdog has become the wolf.

Professor Hayek proposes that a free-market watchdog should be legalised so that good private money might drive out bad government money, if it is bad. There is room for argument whether this would prove more or less effective than, say, control by a revitalised and independent Bank of England; but there can be no dispute whatever that some kind of watchdog must be appointed, and quickly.

HAROLD ROSE

Esmée Fairbairn Professor of Finance, London Graduate School of Business Studies
Economic Adviser to Barclays Bank
Author of *Management Education in the 1970s: Growth and Issues (1969)*

PROFESSOR HAYEK'S prescription involves abolition of all exchange control and allowing exchange rates to move freely. But then it would not be necessary to eliminate the monopolistic title of legal tender as well. For the movement of interest rates and forward exchange rates would fully reflect the degree of trust in different currencies, and the price mechanism would enable contracts to be made to no disadvantage even in a weak currency, thus avoiding all the costs of inconvenience and uncertainty the absence of legal tender would entail.

Put in this way, Professor Hayek's prescription becomes less revolutionary than it sounds, and I have correspondingly less faith in its efficacy. For sustained inflation has not been confined to countries whose governments have surrounded them with the wall of exchange control, and there is in any event nothing to prevent several countries from inflating together, as they have done during the past few years.

Whether governments would in practice be any more ready to affirm their financial virtue by abolishing exchange control than by submitting themselves to more direct financial disciplines, such as the limitation of the money supply, is to be doubted. But Professor Hayek's analysis is undoubtedly correct in pointing to the operation of a kind of Gresham's Law if our inflation continues. Sooner or later the evasion of exchange control will spread; and the ordinary citizen, with no means of defending himself, will have the worst of all worlds.

DOUGLAS JAY, PC, MP

Fellow of All Souls College, Oxford, 1930-37, 1968-
Economic Secretary to the Treasury, 1947-50,
Financial Secretary, 1950-51
President of the Board of Trade, 1964-67
Author of *The Socialist Case (1937)*

IN HIS PAPER, *Choice in Currency,* Professor Hayek seems to have been led astray either by his life-long quarrel with Lord Keynes, or else by the ancient fallacy - now common - of believing that if one system does not yield ideal results, anything else would do better. He wants governments to refrain from declaring anything legal tender, and all individuals to use what money they like. He says that people should be 'free to refuse any money they distrusted and to prefer money in which they had confidence'.

But suppose I offer one paper rouble in payment of a bus fare, and the conductor refuses to accept it; what happens? Is the bus stopped while the conductor and I seek a ruling which nobody can give? And imagine the controversies in the bus over the latest exchange rate between one currency and any other. Professor Hayek's new scheme would produce chaos and slow down the whole business of production and exchange in a welter of disputation. That is why history has forced governments to legislate on legal tender. Professor Hayek might nearly as well ask for the abolition of all law courts and indeed governments, and let every individual prosecute his own disputes. Such an argument has, no doubt, a superficial appeal. But human history argues rather strongly against it.

Of course, Professor Hayek is right in saying that many governments (and banking systems) have for most of history abused their right to issue money. He rather forgets the banking systems. Yet in the Great Barber Credit Inflation of 1972-73 in the UK, it was the banks - tolerated, not instigated, by the Government which engineered the inflation.

But in thinking you can take control of the currency out of the hands of modern elected governments, and put it in the hands of some mysterious wise men meditating in some ivory tower, Professor Hayek is flying in the face of reality. The public simply will not allow control of money to be put beyond their control any more than control of laws or taxes. The only hope, even if a frail one, is to educate governments to act sensibly.

SIR KEITH JOSEPH, BT., PC, MP
Fellow of All Souls College, Oxford, 1946-60, 1972-
Secretary of State for Social Services, Dept. of Health and Social Security, 1970-74
Economic Adviser to Mrs Margaret Thatcher and member of the Shadow Cabinet
Author of *Reversing the Trend (1975)*

PROFESSOR HAYEK'S elegant, penetrating and humane argument will teach most of us that if governments will not cure inflation, then they can at least enable the people to safeguard themselves from the horrors of currency collapse - by allowing a free choice of currency.

No doubt the Treasury would object - on balance of payments and currency control grounds, for, unlike what I understand to be the legality of sterling payments merely indexed to a foreign currency, this would end exchange control. No doubt some politicians and some trade union leaders would object. But voters and wage-earners would not necessarily agree with their nominal spokesmen. They long for a stable medium of exchange and store of value. A minority at all levels of income can and will protect themselves against inflation. Most will not be able to do so. The humanity of Professor Hayek's proposal is that it could partly at least safeguard all our people against the incompetence or irresolution of their own government.

The relevance may become intense if the pending deceleration of inflation proves only to be a false dawn. And anyway the looming obligation to ease exchange control under the EEC rules will before long revive the need to discuss the constraints under which we have become used to living – and the self-correcting mechanisms that would be brought into play by a dose of freedom.

I hope that the implications of Professor Hayek's proposal will be explored so that we may the better judge its potency and potential.

Government Monopoly of Money in Theory and History

Compiled and introduced by
SUDHA SHENOY
Lecturer in Economics, University of Newcastle,
New South Wales, 1973-74
Lecturer in Economics, Cranfield School of Management, 1974-

I. THEORY
(i) *Political Law or Commercial Acceptability?*

Professor Ludwig von Mises made the essential point in this extract: a currency is used as a medium of exchange not *because it is declared to be legal tender but because it is generally acceptable.*

... The law may declare anything it likes to be a medium of payment, and this ruling will be binding on all courts and on all those who enforce the decisions of the courts. But bestowing the property of legal tender on a thing does not suffice to make it money in the economic sense. Goods can become common media of exchange only through the practice of those who take part in commercial transactions; and it is the valuations of these persons alone that determine the exchange-ratios of the market. Quite possibly, commerce may take into use those things to which the state has ascribed the power of payment; but it *need* not do so. It may, if it likes, reject them.

Three situations are possible when the state has declared an object to be a legal means of fulfilling an outstanding obligation. First, the legal means of payment may be identical with the medium of exchange that the contracting parties had in mind when entering into their agreement; or, if not identical, it may yet be of equal value with this medium at the time of payment. For example, the state may proclaim gold as a legal medium for settling obligations contracted in terms of gold, or, at a time when the relative values of gold and silver are as 1 to 15½, it may declare that liabilities in terms of gold may be settled by payment of 15½ times the quantity of silver. Such an arrangement is merely the legal formulation of the presumable intent of the agreement. It damages the interests of neither party. It is economically neutral. The case is otherwise when the state proclaims as medium of payment something that has a higher or lower value than the contractual medium. The first possibility may be disregarded; but the second, of which numerous historical examples could be cited, is important. From the legal point of view, in which the fundamental principle is the protection of vested rights, such a procedure on the part of the state can never be justified, although it might sometimes be vindicated on social or fiscal grounds. But it always means, not the fulfilment of obligations, but their complete or partial cancellation. When notes that are appraised commercially at only half their face-value are proclaimed legal tender, this amounts fundamentally to the same thing as granting debtors legal relief from half of their liabilities.

Depreciation and commercial prudence
State declarations of legal tender affect only those monetary obligations that have already been contracted. But commerce is free to choose between retaining its old medium of exchange or creating a new one for itself, and when it adopts a new medium, so far as the legal power of the contracting parties reaches, it will attempt to make it into a standard of deferred payments also, in order to deprive of its validity, at least for the future, the standard to which the state has ascribed complete powers of debt-settlement. When, during the last decade of the 19th century, the bi-metallist party in Germany gained so much power that the possibility of experiment with its inflationist proposals had to be reckoned with, gold clauses began to make their appearance in long-term contracts. The recent period of currency depreciation has had a similar effect. If the state does not wish to render all credit transactions impossible, it must recognise such devices as these and instruct the courts to acknowledge them. And, similarly, when the state itself enters into ordinary business dealings, when it buys or sells, guarantees loans or borrows, makes payments or receives them, it must recognise the common business medium of exchange as money. The legal standard, the particular group of things that are endued with the property of unlimited legal tender, is in fact valid only for the settlement of existing debts, unless business usage itself adopts it as a general medium of exchange.

(Ludwig von Mises, *Theory of Money and Credit,* Foundation for Economic Education, Irvington-on-Hudson, New York, 1971 reprint of 1953 edition, pp. 70-71.)

(ii) *Bad Money Drives out Good - Gresham's Law or Government Price-Fixing?*

Gresham's Law is usually formulated as bad money driving good out of circulation. But this phenomenon occurs only where the government fixes the exchange rate between the two currencies. As circumstances change, one currency or the other becomes over-valued or under-valued. The under-valued currency then disappears from circulation.

Mintage has long been a prerogative of the rulers of the country. However, this government activity had originally no objective other than the stamping and certifying of weights and measures. The authority's stamp placed upon a piece of metal was supposed to certify its weight and fineness. When later princes resorted to substituting baser and cheaper metals for a part of the precious metals while retaining the customary face and name of the coins, they did it furtively and in full awareness of the fact that they were engaged in a fraudulent attempt to cheat the public. As soon as people found out these artifices, the debased coins were dealt with at a discount as against the old better ones. The governments reacted by resorting to compulsion and coercion. They made it illegal to discriminate in trade and in the settlement of deferred payments between 'good' money and 'bad' money and decreed maximum prices in terms of 'bad' money. However, the result obtained was not that which the governments aimed at. Their decrees failed to stop the process which adjusted commodity prices (in terms of the debased currency) to the actual state of the money relation. Moreover, the effects appeared which Gresham's Law describes.

(Ludwig von Mises, *Human Action*, Regnery, Chicago, Third revised edition, 1966, pp. 780-781.)

Champions of the government's coinage monopoly have claimed that money *is* different from all other commodities, because 'Gresham's Law' proves that 'bad money drives out good' from circulation. Hence, the free market cannot be trusted to serve the public in supplying good money. But this formulation rests on a misinterpretation of Gresham's famous law. The law really says that 'money overvalued artificially by government will drive out of circulation artificially undervalued money'. Suppose, for example, there are 1 ounce gold coins in circulation. After a few years of wear-and-tear, let us say that some coins weigh only 0.9 oz. Obviously, on the free market, the worn coins would circulate at only 90 per cent of the value of the full-bodied coins, and the nominal face-value of the former would have to be repudiated. If anything, *it* will be the 'bad' coins that will be driven from the market. But suppose the government decrees that everyone must treat the worn coins as equal to new, fresh coins, and must accept them equally in payment of debts. What has the government really done? It has imposed *price control* by coercion on the 'exchange rate' between the two types of coin. By insisting on a par-ratio when the worn coins should exchange at a 10 per cent discount, it artificially *overvalues* the worn coins and *undervalues* new coins. Consequently, everyone will circulate the worn coins, and hoard or export the new.

'Bad money drives out good money', then, *not* on the free market, but as the direct result of governmental intervention in the market.

Legal tender.

. . . How was the government able to enforce its price controls on monetary exchange rates? By a device known as *legal tender laws*. Money is used for payment of past debts, as well as for present 'cash' transactions. *With* the name of a country's currency now prominent in accounting instead of *its* actual weight, contracts began to pledge payment in certain amounts of 'money'. *Legal tender laws* dictated what that 'money' could be. When only the original gold or silver was designated 'legal tender', people considered *it* harmless, but they should have realised that a dangerous precedent had been set for government control of money. If the government sticks to the original money, *its* legal tender law is superfluous and unnecessary.[1] On the other hand, the government may declare as legal tender a lower-quality currency side-by-side with the original. Thus, the government may decree worn coins as good as new ones in paying off debt, or silver and gold equivalent to each other in the fixed ratio. The legal tender laws then bring Gresham's Law into being.

(Murray N. Rothbard, *What Has Government Done to Our Money?*, Rampart College, Santa Ana, California, 1974, pp. 9-10, 35.)

---

[1] 'The ordinary law of contract does all that is necessary without any law giving special functions to particular forms of currency. We have adopted a gold sovereign as our unit...If I promise to pay 100 sovereigns, it needs no special currency law of legal tender to say that I am bound to pay 100 sovereigns, and that, if required to pay 100 sovereigns, I cannot discharge my obligation by paying anything else.' (Lord Farrer, *Studies in Currency 1898,* MacMillan and Co. London, 1898, p. 43. On the legal tender laws, see also Mises, *Human Action*, Yale University Press, New Haven, 1949, pp. 432n, 444.)

(iii) *The Solution*

Professor Hayek first advocated the use of alternative currencies in 1960.

Though I am convinced that modern credit banking as it has developed requires some public institutions such as the central banks, I am doubtful whether it is necessary or desirable that they (or the government) should have the *monopoly* of the issue of all kinds of money. The state has, of course, the right to protect the name of the unit of money which it (or anybody else) issues and, if it issues 'dollars', to prevent anybody else from issuing tokens with the same name. And as it is its function to enforce contracts, it must be able to determine what is 'legal tender' for the discharge of any obligation contracted. But there seems to be no reason whatever why the state should ever prohibit the use of *other* kinds of media of exchange, be it some commodity or money issued by another agency, *domestic or foreign*. One of the most effective measures for protecting the freedom of the individual might indeed be to have constitutions *prohibiting* all peacetime restrictions on transactions in any kind of money or the precious metals. (Editorial italics.)

(F. A. Hayek, *The Constitution of Liberty*, University of Chicago Press, Chicago, and Routledge & Kegan Paul, London, 1960, pp. 520-521.)

II. HISTORY
(i) *FRANCE, 1789... Assignats and Legal Tender by Penalty of Death*

This extract is taken from an account of the French experience with the assignats issued after the French Revolution. As larger and larger quantities were issued, their value declined progressively - i.e. prices rose. Attempts at price control failed despite the severest penalties. Since gold and silver coins were also in circulation, the French began to reject assignats in their favour because they retained their value. Professor Andrew Dickson White here chronicles the failure of the French government to force the French to accept assignats at the same value as the metallic currencies.

... As far back as November 1792, the Terrorist associate of Robespierre, St Just, in view of the steady rise in prices of the necessaries of life, had proposed a scheme by which these prices should be established by law, at a rate proportionate to the wages of the working classes. This plan lingered in men's minds, taking shape in various resolutions and decrees until the whole culminated on 29 September, 1793, in the Law of the Maximum.

. . . Committees of experts were appointed to study the whole subject of prices, and at last there were adopted the great 'four rules' which seemed to statesmen of that time a masterly solution of the whole difficulty.

The Law of the Maximum
First, the price of each article of necessity was to be fixed at one and one-third its price in 1790. *Secondly,* all transportation was to be added at a fixed rate per league. *Thirdly,* 5 per cent was to be added for the profit of the wholesaler. *Fourthly,* 10 per cent was to be added for the profit of the retailer. Nothing could look more reasonable. Great was the jubilation. The report was presented and supported by Barrere - 'the tiger monkey' - then in all the glory of his great orations: now best known from his portrait by Macaulay. Nothing could withstand Barrere's eloquence. He insisted that France had been suffering from a *'Monarchical* commerce which only sought wealth', while what she needed and what she was now to receive was a *'Republican* commerce - a commerce of moderate profits and virtuous'. He exulted in the fact that 'France alone enjoys such a commerce - that it exists in no other nation'. He poured contempt over political economy as 'that science which quacks have corrupted, which pedants have obscured, and which academicians have depreciated'. France, he said, has something better, and he declared in conclusion, 'The needs of the people will no longer be spied upon in order that the commercial classes may arbitrarily take advantage'.

The first result of the Maximum was that every means was taken to evade the fixed price imposed, and the farmers brought in as little produce as they possibly could. This increased the scarcity, and the people of the large cities were put on an allowance. Tickets were issued authorising the bearer to obtain at the official prices a certain amount of bread or sugar or soap or wood or coal to cover immediate necessities.

Price-fixing a failure
But it was found that the Maximum, with its divinely revealed four rules, could not be made to work well - even by the shrewdest devices. In the greater part of France it could not be enforced. As to merchandise of

foreign origin or merchandise into which any foreign product entered, the war had raised it far above the price allowed under the first rule, namely, the price of 1790 with an addition of one-third. Shopkeepers therefore could not sell such goods without ruin. The result was that very many went out of business, and the remainder forced buyers to pay enormous charges under the very natural excuse that the seller risked his life in trading at all. That this excuse was valid is easily seen by the daily lists of those condemned to the guillotine, in which not infrequently figure the names of men charged with violating the Maximum laws. Manufactures were very generally crippled and frequently destroyed, and agriculture was fearfully depressed. To detect goods concealed by farmers and shopkeepers, a spy system was established with a reward to the informer of one-third of the value of the goods discovered. To spread terror, the Criminal Tribunal at Strassburg was ordered to destroy the dwelling of anyone found guilty of selling goods above the price set by law. The farmer often found that he could not raise his products at anything like the price required by the new law; and when he tried to hold back his crops or cattle, alleging that he could not afford to sell them at the prices fixed by law, they were frequently taken from him by force and he was fortunate if paid even in the depreciated fiat money - fortunate, indeed, if he finally escaped with his life.

Death for refusal of legal tender

Involved in all these perplexities, the Convention tried to cut the Gordian knot. It decreed that any person selling gold or silver coin, or making any difference in any transaction between paper and specie, should be imprisoned in irons for six years; that anyone who refused to accept a payment in assignats, or accepted assignats at a discount, should pay a fine of 3,000 francs; and that anyone committing this crime a second time should pay a fine of 6,000 francs and suffer imprisonment 20 years in irons. Later, on 8 September, 1793, the penalty for such offences was made death, with confiscation of the criminal's property, and a reward was offered to any person informing the authorities regarding any such criminal transaction. To reach the climax of ferocity, the Convention decreed, in May 1794, that the death penalty should be inflicted on any person convicted of 'having asked, before a bargain was concluded, in what money payment was to be made'. Nor was this all. The great finance minister, Cambon, soon saw that the worst enemies of his policy were gold and silver. Therefore it was that, under his lead, the Convention closed the Exchange and finally, on 13 November, 1793, under terrifying penalties, suppressed all commerce in the precious metals.

... All this vast chapter in financial folly is sometimes referred to as if it resulted from the direct action of men utterly unskilled in finance. This is a grave error. That wild schemers and dreamers took a leading part in setting the fiat money system going is true; that speculation and interested financiers made it worse is also true; but the men who had charge of French finance during the Reign of Terror and who made these experiments, which seem to us so monstrous, in order to rescue themselves and their country from the flood which was sweeping everything to financial ruin were universally recognised as among the most skilful and honest financiers in Europe. Cambon, especially, ranked then and ranks now as among the most expert in any period. The disastrous results of all his courage and ability in the attempt to stand against the deluge of paper money show how powerless are the most skilful masters of finance to stem the tide of fiat money calamity when once it is fairly under headway; and how useless are all enactments which they can devise against the underlying laws of nature.

Month after month, year after year, new issues went on. Meanwhile, everything possible was done to keep up the value of paper. The city authorities of Metz took a solemn oath that the assignats should bear the same price whether in paper or specie, and whether in buying or selling, and various other official bodies throughout the nation followed this example. In obedience to those who believed with the market women of Paris, as stated in their famous petition, that 'laws should be passed making paper money as good as gold', Couthon, in August 1793, had proposed and carried a law punishing any person who should sell assignats at less than their nominal value with imprisonment for 20 years in chains, and later carried a law making investments in foreign countries by Frenchmen punishable with death.

'Fiat' money obeyed natural laws of finance
But to the surprise of the great majority of the French people, the value of the assignats was found, after the momentary spasm of fear had passed, not to have been permanently increased by these measures. On the contrary, this 'fiat' paper persisted in obeying the natural laws of finance and, as new issues increased, their value decreased.

... The issues of paper money continued. Toward the end of 1794 seven thousand millions in assignats were in circulation. By the end of May 1795, the circulation was increased to ten thousand millions; at the end of July, to fourteen thousand millions; and the value of one hundred francs in paper fell steadily, first to four francs in gold, then to three, then to two and one-half.

The powerless guillotine and the power of gold
. . . Interesting is it to note in the midst of all this the steady action of another simple law in finance. Prisons, guillotines, enactments inflicting 20 years' imprisonment in chains upon persons twice convicted of buying or selling paper money at less than its nominal value, and death upon investors in foreign securities, were powerless. The National Convention, fighting a world in arms and with an armed revolt on its own soil, showed titanic power, but in its struggle to circumvent one simple law of nature its weakness was pitiable. The *louis d'or* stood in the market as a monitor, noting each day, with unerring fidelity, the decline in value of the assignat; a monitor not to be bribed, not to be scared. As well might the National Convention try to bribe or scare away the polarity of the mariner's compass. On 1 August, 1795, this gold louis of 25 francs was worth in paper, 920 francs; on 1 September, 1,200 francs; on 1 November, 2,600 francs; on 1 December, 3,050 francs. In February 1796, it was worth 7,200 francs or one franc in gold was worth 288 francs in paper. Prices of all commodities went up nearly in proportion.

(Andrew Dickson White, *Fiat Money: Inflation in France*, Foundation for Economic Education, Irvington-on-Hudson, New York, 1959, pp. 75-89; first published in 1912 as revised version of 1876 lecture.)

(ii) *USA, before 1857 (five foreign currencies legal tender) and after (only the dollar)*

The United States up to the 1850s offers an important historical instance of the use of a wide variety of currencies. Dutch, English, French, Portuguese, and Spanish coins circulated freely as legal tender. Prices were quoted in Spanish dollars. After 1834 increasing quantities of American coins were minted, and in 1857 foreign coins were declared to be legal tender no longer.

(Based on Ernest L. Bogart and Donald L. Kemmerer, *An Economic History of the American People*, Longmans Green and Co, New York, 1942, pp. 360-361; and Hermann E. Knooss, *American Economic Development*, Prentice Hall, Englewood Cliffs, N.J., 1974, pp. 271-272.)

(iii) GERMANY, 1920-23

We now take two extracts from Professor Constantino Bresciani-Turroni's book, The Economics of Inflation, *on the great German inflation of 1920-23. Together, they illustrate how foreign currencies, and a host of illegal monies, replaced the hyper-inflated paper mark, in the last stages of the inflation. These alternative currencies were replaced, in turn, by the stabilised rentenmark. Although the hyper-inflated mark was legal tender, it was eventually rejected by the Germans. Its rejection forced the government to stabilise the currency.*

Professor Bresciani-Turroni here describes how substantial quantities of foreign exchange and various illegal paper currencies began to circulate in Germany towards the end of the inflation. As there were no quantitative restraints on these illegal monies, they too depreciated in value. But they continued to be accepted in preference to the mark, which was depreciating even faster. Before the issue of the stabilised rentenmark (in November 1923), emergency notes were introduced, printed with the words 'stable value'. The phrase was fictitious, but by now the Germans were ready to accept any currency other than the hyper-inflated mark.

In this last phase the legal paper money was replaced by other monies (which had no legal recognition), not only as 'a store of value' and as 'a standard of value', but also as a means of payment. Little by little foreign money, or the old national metallic money (which had been hoarded), or new money created by private firms, entered the circulation. The legal money was rejected by the public. . . .

The replacements of the legal money by other monies in Germany developed in an interesting way. In the summer of 1922, at a time when the external value of the mark was falling rapidly, causing a revolution of internal prices, the most important industries, one after another, adopted the practice of expressing prices in a foreign 'appreciated' money (dollars, Swiss francs, Dutch florins, etc.) or in gold marks. . . . Later the paper mark continually lost importance as a means of payment also. Wholesale trade, which badly needed a means of payment, resorted to foreign exchange.

In the summer of 1923, the need for a circulating medium being at times very acute, because of the rapid fall in the total real value of paper marks, the 'emergency monies' (which had from time to time appeared in the circulation... regulated by the law of 17 July, 1922) were multiplied. State and local governments, industrial associations, chambers of commerce, and private traders issued great quantities of paper 'money'. Sometimes the issues were authorised and came under certain guarantees (see the decree of 26 October, 1923), but most were illegal issues, which, thanks to the rapid depreciation of notes, yielded considerable profits to the issuers. Illegal issues were especially frequent in the occupied territories. It is said that in the autumn of 1923 there were two thousand different kinds of emergency money in circulation! The abuses which arose from these issues constitute one of the most unhappy chapters in the history of the mark.

From the mark to the rentenmark
Towards mid-October 1923 it was obvious that the monetary chaos could not go on any longer without involving the entire economic system in complete catastrophe. On 13 October the law granting full powers was passed, and on 15 October the decree which instituted the 'Rentenbank' provided for the issue of a new money, the rentenmark, beginning from 15 November, 1923.

But, in the meantime, among the German population the need for a stable-value currency had become greater than ever. The working classes especially declared further delays to be intolerable and imperiously demanded a means of payment with *a stable value*. It being impossible, for technical reasons, to anticipate the date of the issue of the rentenmark, it was necessary to look elsewhere for an immediate solution of the urgent monetary problem, in order to avoid the dangers arising from the threatening attitude of the working classes. The Government put into circulation some small denominations (up to a tenth of a dollar) of 'Gold Loan' and some 'Dollar Treasury Bonds'. However, as the notes immediately available were very limited, the Government authorised and even encouraged the issue of 'emergency monies with a constant value' (wertbeständiges Notgeld).

The issuers - who were principally the provinces, towns, and chambers of commerce - had to cover completely the paper money issued by depositing an equivalent sum in Gold Loan securities or by a special type of Gold Treasury Bond, which was created for the purpose (see decree of 26 October, 1923, and successive modifications, published by the Press on 4 November).

The railway administration was authorised to issue 'emergency monies with a constant value', up to the amount of 200 million gold marks, which were 'guaranteed' by a deposit of Gold Loan and of Gold Treasury Bonds of equivalent value.

It is unnecessary to state that *the guarantee of the so-called 'money with a stable value' was purely fictitious*. Actually the Gold Loan and the Gold Treasury Bonds were mere paper without any cover. (Editorial italics.)

Indeed, the law of 14 August, 1923, on the Gold Loan of 500 million gold marks, contained only this limited promise:

> 'In order to guarantee the payment of interest and the redemption of the loan of 500 million gold marks, the Government of the Reich is authorised, if the ordinary receipts do not provide sufficient cover, to raise supplements to the tax on capital, in accordance with detailed regulations to be determined later.'

These vague words constituted the entire guarantee behind the Gold Loan! Nevertheless, the Gold Loan Bonds and the notes issued against the Gold Loan deposits did not depreciate in value. The public allowed itself to be hypnotised by the word 'wertbeständig; (stable-value) written on the new paper money. And the public accordingly accepted and hoarded these notes (the Gold Loan Bonds almost disappeared from circulation) even whilst it rejected the old paper mark - preferring not to trade rather than receive a currency in which it had lost all faith.[1]

Rejection of legal tender

Together with the introduction of foreign currencies and exchange, the creation of the 'emergency money' (which became important in the German circulation in the autumn of 1923 - indeed, the total value of the emergency money became considerably higher than the total value of the legal tender money) was evidence of *the spontaneous reaction of the economic organism against the depreciation of the legal currency.*[2] (Editorial italics.)

---

[1] It is not possible to estimate the value of the 'emergency money' which circulated in Germany just before the introduction of the rentenmark, because the illegal issues cannot be estimated. According to official estimates, the *authorised* 'Notgeld' and 'Goldanleihe' amounted to 728 million gold marks on 31 December, 1923. According to an estimate of the Statistical Bureau of the Reich (see *Wirtschaft und Statistik*, 1924, p.121) the issue of unauthorised subsidiary money amounted, at its maximum, to 332 trillion paper marks. In its *Report* for 1923 the Reichsbank gave a considerably higher figure: 400-500 trillion paper marks.

[2] According to Professor Hirsch the phenomenon of the 'repudiation' of the paper mark was clearly apparent towards the end of June 1923, at first in the occupied territory and later in other parts of Germany. Instead the 'Goldanleihe' was accepted by the country people. A considerable part of the harvest of 1923

It is impossible to show in any precise fashion the amount of foreign exchange circulating in Germany before the introduction of the rentenmark. Estimates vary very much. According to an estimate of the Cuno Government the foreign exchange and currencies in Germany in December 1922 amounted to 3 milliard gold marks. But the amount effectively circulating is not known. Accepting the opinion of some business men, Schacht estimated in October 1923 at 1.5 to 2 milliards the amount of foreign exchange and currencies circulating in Germany. According to Professor Hirsch, in the inflation years much foreign money entered Germany, part being hoarded and part being used as a means of payment. He maintains that this reserve of exchange in the autumn of 1923 was worth between three and four milliard gold marks. However, all these estimates are unreliable.

(C. Bresciani-Turroni, *The Economics of Inflation*, Augustus M. Kelley, New York, 1968 reprint of 1937 edition, pp. 341-345.)

The rentenmark was accepted only because its issue was strictly limited. It replaced not the old hyper-inflated mark but all the 'emergency monies' issued in the last stages of the hyper-inflation as well as the foreign exchange also circulating illegally.

... In October and in the first half of November [1923] lack of confidence in the German legal currency was such that, as Luther wrote, 'any piece of paper, however problematical its guarantee, on which was written "constant value" was accepted more willingly than the paper mark'.

... But on the basis of the simple fact that the new paper money [the rentenmark] had a different name from the old, the public thought it was something different from the paper mark, believed in the efficacy of the mortgage guarantee and had confidence. The new money was accepted, despite the fact it was an inconvertible paper currency. It was held and not spent rapidly, as had happened in the last months with the paper mark.

---

was bought by consumers with Gold Loan securities (*Die deutsche Währungsfrage*, Berlin, 1924, pp. 121, 129). But in the cities, as the present author discovered personally, the paper mark was not rejected, although the 'appreciated' foreign currencies were more willingly accepted.

Confidence in rentenmark dependent on limited issue

Undoubtedly this confidence, thanks to which the rentenmark could enter the channels of circulation immediately, would have been quickly dissipated if the public had been led to expect that, despite the obligation imposed on the Rentenbank by decree, the Government would exceed the pre-arranged limit to issues.[1] An attempt to violate these obligations was made by the Government in December 1923, but it was confronted by a determined refusal by the management of the Rentenbank. The incident helped to strengthen confidence in the new money. The limitation of the quantity was then of primary and fundamental importance.

... the rentenmark and the new paper marks took the place of the various auxiliary monies, legal and illegal, which had been issued in the autumn of 192], and of foreign exchange.

In fact, from German monetary statistics it appears that the circulation of the 'Notgeld' and of the 'Goldanleihe' notes fell continually after the introduction of the rentenmark. The amount of authorised emergency money, of railway emergency money and of Gold Loan notes in circulation, which was 728 million gold marks on 31 December, 1923, was reduced to 348 millions on 31 March, 1924, and to 38 millions on 31 July following.

At the same time the Reichsbank energetically set about eliminating illegal emergency monies from circulation. According to an inquiry made by the Central Statistical Bureau, at the end of January 1924, the circulation of unauthorised money was reduced to about 160 trillions (132 of which were in occupied territory) and to 105.6 trillions at the end of February of the same year.

... The increase in the circulation of legal money which occurred after the introduction of the rentenmark can be explained, up to the amount of 1,100-1,200 million marks, by the substitution of rentenmarks and paper marks for the various kinds of auxiliary monies.[2]

The phenomenon of the replacement of foreign exchange by German money showed itself in the balance sheets of the Reichsbank, which showed a continuous and noticeable rise in the item 'other assets', in which, as

---

[1] According to the Decree of 15 October, 1923, the maximum issue of rentenmarks was fixed at 2,400 million, including 1,200 million to be put at the disposal of the Government.

[2] According to the statements made by the President of the Reichsbank on 26 May, 1924, at Hamburg, on 1 January, 1924, there were still 1,157 million gold marks of auxiliary money circulating in Germany; at the end of May of the same year it was reduced to 152 million.

experts know, was included precisely that foreign exchange. It shows that the public sold foreign exchange to the Reichsbank for German money.

(C. Bresciani-Turroni, *ibid.*, pp. 347-349.)

AND A PORTENT...?
Currency option for foreign creditors*

THE HOUSE of Lords decided yesterday that foreign creditors should not suffer in English courts from the combination of sterling's falling exchange rate and the ancient procedural rule that English courts can award money payments only in sterling.

By a majority of four to one, the Law Lords ruled that in English courts, foreign creditors could now have their claims recognised in their own currencies.

The decision is of great significance for trade, improving the prospects for foreign creditors facing the possibility of litigation in English courts. But the very breadth of issues involved led Lord Simon of Glaisdale to dissent. He held that the issue was unsuitable for judicial reform as it required a wide range of official and commercial advice.

Fluctuations

The Law Lords confirmed the view that world currency fluctuations called for a change which would enable the foreign creditor to get what he bargained for in his contract - a view taken for the first time by the Court of Appeal with Lord Denning presiding, in *Schorsch Meier 'D. Hennin* in November 1974.

They dismissed an appeal by George Frank (Textiles) of London, against a Court of Appeal decision of 10 February that they must pay their Swiss supplier, Michael Miliangos, Payerne, in Swiss francs.

When the case was heard before Mr Justice Bristow in the High Court last December, the British company did not dispute the liability to pay for textiles delivered in 1972, but they did contend that payment should be made in sterling. The judge accepted this view and delivered a judgement for £42,038 - the 1972 equivalent of the invoice in Swiss francs. This was about £18,000 less than was necessary to buy the same sum in Swiss francs at the exchange rate of the day when the case was decided.

---

* Reproduced with permission from *The Financial Times*, 6 November, 1975.

The decision was however reversed by the Court of Appeal and the reversal has now been confirmed on further appeal to the Lords. The Swiss supplier will recover his claim undiminished by currency changes and the British importer will pay about £30,000 more than he would have paid in 1972, plus legal costs which are likely to double this amount.

Giving judgement, Lord Edmund-Davies said that to apply the old rule to the present case would perpetrate a great injustice.

Lord Cross of Chelsea said that the change in the foreign exchange situation and the position of sterling over the last 15 years justified the House in overturning the old rule.

Lord Wilberforce said that a creditor should not suffer from sterling fluctuation.

Choice in Currency
F. A. HAYEK

1. The chief root of monetary troubles is the scientific authority the Keynesians gave the superstition that increasing the quantity of money can ensure prosperity and full employment.

2. The superstition was fought successfully by economists for two centuries of stable prices during the age of modern industrialism and the gold standard.

3. Before then inflation largely dominated history.

4. Keynes's (macro-economic) error was to suppose that labour demand and supply can be equated (and unemployment avoided) by managing *total* demand. Employment depends on demand *in each sector* of the economy. Managing total demand by expanding money supply creates only temporary and therefore unstable employment.

5. A 'lost generation' of economists who have learned nothing else continues to offer the quack 'full employment' remedy and to win short-term popularity for it.

6. No government, national or international, that wants to remain in office can be expected to limit the quantity of money better than a gold standard or any other (semi-) automatic system because in practice it succumbs to sectional pressures for additional cheap money and expenditure.

7. The gold standard, balanced budgets, fixed exchanges, enabled governments to resist sectional importunities. The removal of these 'shackles' has enabled governments to act more irresponsibly.

8. The only hope for stable money and resistance to inflation is to protect money from politics by removing the power of government to require its citizens to use its money as the *only* legal tender.

9. Government would then not inflate its supply, because it would be forsaken for other currencies.

10. Inflation can therefore be stopped by introducing competition in currency. The notion that it is a proper function of government to issue the national currency is false. Citizens should be free to use and refuse any currencies they wish: politicians would then have to limit their quantities. Then inflation would be avoided.

LargePrintLiberty.com

Dedicated to offering books on libertarian thought and economics in Large Print paperback.

Titles include:

For a New Liberty, by Murray N. Rothbard (Philosophy)
"A classic that for over two decades has been hailed as the best general work on libertarianism available. Rothbard begins with a quick overview of its historical roots, and then goes on to define libertarianism as resting 'upon one single axiom: that no man or group of men shall aggress upon the person or property of anyone else.' He writes a withering critique of the chief violator of liberty: the State. Rothbard then provides penetrating libertarian solutions for many of today's most pressing problems, including poverty, war, threats to civil liberties, the education crisis, and more."

Principles of Economics, by Carl Menger (Economics)
"In the beginning, there was Menger. It was this book that reformulated, and really rescued, economic science. It kicked off the Marginalist Revolution, which corrected theoretical errors of the old classical school. These errors concerned value theory, and they had sown enough confusion to make the dangerous ideology of Marxism seem more plausible than it really was. Menger set out to elucidate the precise nature of economic value, and root economics firmly in the real-world actions of individual human beings."

Great Wars and Great Leaders, by Ralph Raico (History)
"In the backdrop of this blistering and deeply insightful and scholarly history is the whitewashing of 'great leaders' like Woodrow Wilson, Winston Churchill, FDR, Truman, Stalin, Trotsky, and other collectivists. They are highly regarded because they were on the 'right side' of the rise of the state. But do they deserve adulation? Raico says no: these great leaders were main agents in the decline of civilization in the 20th century, all of them anti-liberals who used their power to celebrate and enhance state power."

www.ingramcontent.com/pod-product-compliance
Lightning Source LLC
Chambersburg PA
CBHW081907170526
45167CB00007B/3193